BEHIND THE NEWS

UPRISINGS IN THE MIDDLE EAST

Philip Steele

WAYLAND

First published in 2014 by Wayland

Copyright © Wayland 2014

Wayland
338 Euston Road
London NW1 3BH

Wayland Australia
Level 17/207 Kent Street
Sydney, NSW 2000

All Rights Reserved.
Produced for Wayland by Tall Tree Ltd
Editors: Emma Marriott and Jon Richards
Designer: Malcolm Parchment

ISBN 978 0 7502 8255 0
E-book ISBN 978 0 7502 8818 7

Dewey number: 303.6'4'0956-dc23

10 9 8 7 6 5 4 3 2 1

Printed in China

Wayland is a division of Hachette Children's
Books, an Hachette UK company
www.hachette.co.uk

The publisher would would like to thank the
following for their kind permission to reproduce
their photographs:

Shutterstock.com unless stated otherwise:
Front cover: Oleg Zabielin, E_Mike, Hang Dinh
© Mohamed Hanno (4), WIki_Commons public
domain (6), Philip Lange (7), © Rraheb (8), © STR/
epa/Corbis (9), © Richard Gunion (11), © Smandy (11),
© Mohamed Elsayyed (13), Nataliya Hora (13),
WIki_Commons public domain (14), David Burrows
(15), Mohamed Elsayyed (17), 360b (17), Ryan
Rodrick Beiler (18), Mohamed Elsayyed (19),
leolintang (20), Yevgenia Gorbulsky (21), © Andrew
Chittock (23), meunierd (24), © Smandy (25), Hang
Dinh (26), © Idealink Photography/Alamy (27),
WIki_Commons public domain (29), © ZACARIAS
GARCIA/epa/Corbis (29), Dona_Bozzi (31),
Ryan Rodrick Beiler (32), Vasily Smirnov (33),
Dona_Bozzi (35), Dona_Bozzi (35),
© Leungphotography (37), ChameleonsEye (38),
© Richard Harvey (39), ZouZou (41), WIki_Commons
public domain (41), xdrew (42), © Richard Harvey
(43), fpolat69 (44), © Smandy (45)

CONTENTS

CHANGING TIMES

There are times when oppressive governments begin to lose their grip on power. People gather in streets and squares with a feeling of rising hope. There have been protests, and even uprisings. Now we can look back. Were the protests all in vain?

Arab Spring

Rolling revolutions happened across Europe in 1830 and 1848, and again when the Cold War came to an end in 1989. From 2010 onwards, ideas of revolution and change swept across southwest Asia and North Africa. This series of uprisings became known as the 'Arab Spring' – although not all the people involved were Arabs.

It all began in Tunisia with a single act of protest by Mohammed Bouazizi (see page 10), and soon one extraordinary event was following another. It became difficult to control or predict the outcome. Changes are still taking place throughout the region today. We see them on the news and in the headlines. The images are often of violence and refugees fleeing. Nobody can be sure how it will end.

Egyptian protestors gather in the city of Alexandria demanding the resignation of the then president, Hosni Mubarak.

Making sense of it

This book aims to go behind the news and ask questions. Why is the Middle East so important to those who live in other parts of the world? Why are these changes happening now? Who is taking part and what do they want? Which other countries are influencing events? We have witnessed the hope of young people in those early days. Can that spirit possibly survive?

TIDE OF CHANGE
2010-2014

- **Governments overthrown:** Egypt (twice), Libya, Tunisia, Yemen
- **Wars:** Libya, Syria
- **Protests leading to government changes:** Kuwait, Morocco, Oman, Palestine
- **Protests:** Algeria, Bahrain, Djibouti, Lebanon, Mauritania, Saudi Arabia, Sudan
- **Related crises:** Iran, Iraq, Israel, Mali, Turkey

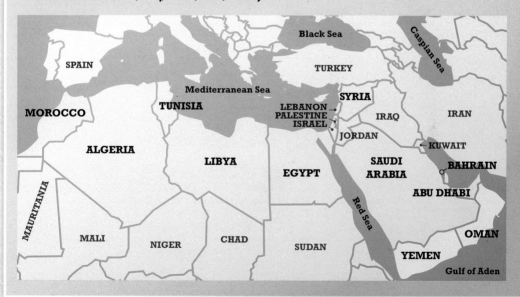

'I think that all of us share and cherish the idea of being free and not afraid anymore.'

Nouha Tourki, a teacher from Tunisia, speaking to the BBC in 2011.

A HISTORY OF UPRISINGS

The Middle East has been always been a region of trade, commerce, religions and ideas, and a crossroads for three continents. Today's problems are rooted in the area's rich and restless history.

Empires and religions

• Between about 9500 and 2250 BCE, the region saw the rise of civilisation, and of farming, cities and great empires.
• Three religions developed in Western Asia between about 1300 BCE and 632 CE – Judaism, Christianity and Islam.
• Arab empires spread Islam across the region from the 600s to the 1200s. From 1096 to 1303, there were Crusades – 'holy wars' between Muslims and European Christians.

Defeated Christian soldiers, known as Crusaders, lay down their weapons to the victorious Muslim leader, Saladin.

The Ottoman Empire

• In 1453, a group of Turks called the Ottomans captured the city now known as Istanbul. At its height in the 1500s and 1600s, the Ottoman Empire controlled much of Western Asia, North Africa and Southeast Europe.

• As European nations became more powerful, the Ottoman Empire went into decline. In the 1800s and 1900s, France, Spain, Italy and Britain seized control or won influence across North Africa.

• In 1914, the Ottoman Empire joined with Germany and Austria to fight in World War I. The British helped the Arabs to revolt against Ottoman rule. The Ottoman Empire was defeated in 1918 and lost its foreign territories. In 1922, it was replaced by the Republic of Turkey.

The modern Middle East

• The Arabs did not win their promised freedom when World War I ended. Under an international agreement, the French ruled in Syria and Lebanon, and the British took control in Palestine. Palestine was partitioned in 1947, to create a new Jewish state which became known as Israel.

• The countries of the region struggled to win independence from the 1920s until the 1960s. Some corrupt monarchies were swept away, but new dictatorships arose in their place.

• From the 1960s, oil wealth transformed Saudi Arabia, Iran, Iraq and Libya. From the 1940s onwards, the region has been repeatedly torn apart by terrorism and by regional and international wars.

Oil fields across the Middle East, such as this one in Bahrain, have made many of the region's countries incredibly wealthy.

UNREST ACROSS THE REGION

In 2010, rising prices, unemployment, corruption and oppression were making life difficult in Tunisia. People wanted the right to vote in fair elections and to speak freely. To everybody's surprise, the power of so many people protesting on the streets proved irresistible. The old political systems began to collapse.

A patchwork of peoples

There was a new common purpose across the region, but there were many differences, too. The Middle East is a patchwork of different peoples, faiths and cultures. The region is home to, among others, Arabs, Berbers, Jews, Turks, Kurds and Iranians. Islam is the largest religion, but it is divided between the followers of the Sunni and Shi'a branches. The other traditional faiths are also divided. The types of government targeted in the Arab Spring vary from traditional monarchies to dictatorships.

A young man holds a sign that says 'People Demand a new Constitution' during anti-government protests in Tahrir Square, Cairo, Egypt.

What kind of future?

Some people wanted a more secular society, in which religious affairs were separated from the state. They wanted more social freedoms such as those in Western countries. Other people were more inspired by the Islamic faith in their search for a new social order. Women from all factions played a big part in the protests. Most people agreed that they wanted change and prosperity – but could they share a vision of the future?

A political earthquake

The ongoing political unrest put a great strain on long-standing tensions within many Middle Eastern countries. It also wrong-footed the governments of the powerful countries that had been influencing politics in the region for so long. How could they protect their interests? Should they get involved?

In 2010, Tunisian rapper El Général performed Rais Lebled ('To the President'), a song about the injustice in the country. The song became the anthem of the Arab Spring.

'Mr President, your people are dying
People are eating rubbish
Look at what is happening
Miseries everywhere, Mr President
I talk with no fear
Although I know I will get only trouble
I see injustice everywhere...'

Rais Lebled ('To the President'), a 2010 song by Tunisian rapper El Général. It was addressed to Tunisian President Ben Ali and became the hip hop anthem of the Arab Spring, from Egypt to Bahrain.

TUNISIA, 2010-2014

Sidi Bouzid is a city in central Tunisia. There, in December 2010, a protest took place when a man called Mohammed Bouazizi set himself on fire. A university graduate, Bouazizi made his living selling vegetables, and had been given a hard time by officials. He later died from his burns.

Tunisia in North Africa was home to 10.9 million people in 2014. It was here that the Arab Spring started.

TUNISIA

NEWS FLASH

Name: Tunisian Republic
Area: 163,610 km²
Capital: Tunis
Ethnic groups: Arab, Berber or Turkish descent (98%), also European and Jewish
Languages: Arabic, also Shilha and French
Religions: Islam (98%), also Christianity and Judaism
The back story:
• Protectorate of France from 1881 to 1956.
• President Habib Bourguiba ruled the country as a one-party state for 31 years.
• Zine el Abidine Ben Ali ruled from 1987.

The first revolution

This single act triggered the Arab Spring. In a pattern that would repeat itself across the region in the coming months, protestors throughout Tunisia poured into streets to complain about rising prices, corruption and human rights abuses.

President Ben Ali had been in power for 23 years, but within a month he was removed from office. Ben Ali fled to Saudi Arabia and the Tunisians rejoiced. However, the Tunisians continued to protest until all elements of the previous government had gone.

In Washington DC, supporters of the Arab Spring protests held up a list of the leaders (described as 'tyrants') they wanted to see removed from power, headed by Tunisia's Ben Ali.

A fresh start?

An election was held in October 2011. The outcome was a coalition government led by the moderate Islamist party Ennahda. Ennahda was soon criticised by the secularists for being too easy on the Salafists, Sunni Muslim puritans who wanted to bring in the Islamic legal system known as Shari'a (see page 20). In turn, many Islamists criticised Ennahda for being too secular.

Amid growing tensions, the political parties agreed that Mehdi Jomas would act as prime minister. A new progressive constitution was introduced in 2014 and elections were planned for later that year.

A young woman proudly waves the Tunisian flag as she makes her way to a polling station during Tunisia's free elections.

'The people think that the problems will simply disappear after a revolution. But they don't, they only change.'

Tunisian President Moncef Marzouki, interviewed by *Deutsche Welle*, March 2013.

ARE PROTESTS ALWAYS VIOLENT?

All the uprisings of the Arab Spring provoked violence, and some turned into long and bloody wars. What surprised many people, including those taking part, was how the first relatively peaceful public demonstrations in Tunisia and Egypt brought real results.

DEBATE Should political protest be non-violent?

YES

The campaigner for Indian independence, Mohandas K Gandhi (1869–1948), successfully used non-violent protest against the British in the 1930s and 40s. Only the moral force of non-violence can bring fundamental and lasting peace.

NO

Gandhi's campaign for Indian independence from British rule could not prevent violence in the end, and the Arab Spring turned violent, too. Just how effective can non-violence be against a really brutal regime?

Powerful forces

When the uprisings occurred across the Middle East, why were they so explosive and volatile? Many activists seen as troublemakers by the authorities had been jailed or banned for decades.

Oppression builds up huge pressures in society, which can turn to violence at times of crisis. Similar forces and fractures have also been unleashed throughout European history, during many uprisings, revolutions and religious wars.

A wounded man is carried away following violent clashes between protestors and security forces in Egypt in November 2011.

Back to basics

In reporting on the Middle East, television news channels often focus on religious divisions, on violence, and on the manoeuvrings of political parties. When asking 'why?' they often ignore the most basic issue – the fact that people want a living wage and security on the streets. In some countries, radical Islamists have won support by providing free food at neighbourhood level. It may be difficult for governments to provide economic solutions on a bigger scale when times are hard, but their survival may depend on it.

A homeless man begs on the street in Midoun, Djerba, Tunisia. High levels of poverty and homelessness increased the feelings of frustration in the run-up to the Arab Spring.

> '... for the majority of Tunisians, the important questions are bread, water, electricity and economic development.'
>
> Tunisian President Moncef Marzouki.

DICTATORSHIP AND DEMOCRACY

For many centuries, countries in southwest Asia and North Africa were under the rule of the Ottoman Turks and then European empires. Struggles for independence were often followed by governments that suppressed human and civil rights.

A changing society

The restless mood of the Arab Spring reflected huge social changes. In countries such as Tunisia, young men and women were now more educated than their parents.

Many were well qualified but were frustrated because they could find few jobs to match their skills. Repressive governance by old men was not for them. Even in the home, traditional, strict family structures were beginning to break down.

Having seized power in 1969, Muammar Gaddafi ruled Libya as a dictatorship until he was overthrown in 2011.

Demanding a voice

Young people saw themselves more as individuals and wanted choices in the way they lived. They demanded a system in which leaders were held to account and their rights were respected. One of the most common words to be heard on the street was 'democracy' – government by fairly elected representatives of the people. The protestors did not share a common political programme, but they all wanted a better quality of life.

Islam, the largest religion in the region, was also in a restless state, full of fervour and debate. The majority of people in the region wanted government with an Islamic dimension, but held very different views about how the faith should engage with political systems.

Many views, one state?

One aim of democratic government is to reconcile multiple or pluralist views within society. Would the uprisings bring people together or drive them apart?

> ## 'In the past, I only focused on personal dreams, but now I'm focusing on a national dream that we all share.'
>
> **Egyptian student Ahmed Raafat Amin, BBC News website.**

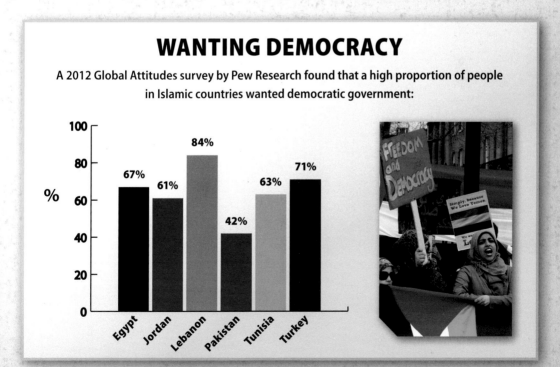

WANTING DEMOCRACY

A 2012 Global Attitudes survey by Pew Research found that a high proportion of people in Islamic countries wanted democratic government:

Country	%
Egypt	67%
Jordan	61%
Lebanon	84%
Pakistan	42%
Tunisia	63%
Turkey	71%

EGYPT, 2011–2014

Cairo is the biggest city in North Africa. It stands on the banks of the River Nile, a short distance from the ancient pyramids of Giza. At its centre is Tahrir ('Liberation') Square, which became a global symbol of the Arab Spring.

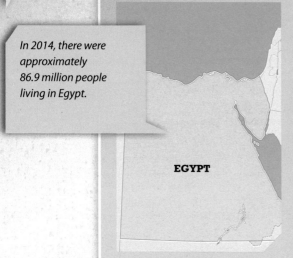

In 2014, there were approximately 86.9 million people living in Egypt.

EGYPT

NEWS FLASH

Name: Arab Republic of Egypt
Area: 1,001,450 km^2
Capital: Cairo
Ethnic groups: Egyptian 99.6%
Language: Arabic
Religions: Islam (90%), Coptic Christianity (9%), other Christianity (1%)
The back story:
• In 1952, Colonel Nasser seized power.
• Egypt was defeated in wars against Israel, but took control of the Suez Canal in 1956.
• President Anwar Sadat made peace with Israel in 1979, but was assassinated in 1981. He was succeeded by Hosni Mubarak.

The people rise

In January 2011, about 50,000 protestors gathered in Tahrir Square, inspired by the news from Tunisia. Within days, that number had swollen to more than 300,000, some said perhaps a million. Soon, protests spread to other cities.

The public mood was excited by the possibility that change was at hand.

President Hosni Mubarak had held power for nearly 30 years. He had imprisoned people without trial, built secret detention centres and failed to tackle corruption. He was now accused

Thousands of people packed into Tahrir Square, setting up makeshift camps, to protest against Mubarak's' regime.

'We are so furious. We must have change, better chances to work, to buy a flat and have just the life's basics.'

Protester in Tahrir Square, *The Guardian*, 2011.

of allowing violent attacks to be made against the protestors. After just 18 days, Mubarak was forced to resign. He handed over power to the army, and was arrested.

An experiment in democracy

In June 2012, the first truly democratic election in Egypt's history was narrowly won by Mohammed Morsi for Freedom and Justice, a party founded by the Islamist Muslim Brotherhood. Morsi was believed by many Western leaders to be a moderate, but he gave himself new powers and proposed a divisive constitution. Protestors returned to Tahrir Square.

The second downfall

The army was back in favour with the crowds. In June 2013, Morsi was forced from office and arrested. The army promised new elections, but the Muslim Brotherhood was banned. Some said the army was safeguarding the revolution. Others complained that this was a military coup. In March 2014, 529 supporters of the Muslim Brotherhood were sentenced to death. There was no jury, no defence and the trial lasted two hours. Reconciliation was no longer on the agenda.

Hosni Mubarak was sentenced to life imprisonment, but this sentence was overturned. He was then freed but placed under house arrest.

IS DEMOCRACY ALWAYS GOOD?

Democracy is never an easy option. If you have taken part in an uprising, it may be hard to hand over power to a rival party that has won an election. The challenges faced by new democracies after the Arab Spring are not unique. Democracy has had to deal with conflict, violence and civil wars in many other regions.

People and power

Democracy has taken many different forms since it first developed in Greece about 2,500 years ago. It remains a far-from-perfect system. It may allow people to choose how they are governed, but it does not always follow that the people's choice will be wise or even moral. Even when a democracy is long established, it may need to be rethought or reformed. This process can raise all sorts of ethical questions. Is democracy always good and dictatorship always wrong? Can a dictator ever do good things for a country? Should a political party be allowed to stand for election if it has an undemocratic programme? Back in 1991, Algeria held its first multi-party elections. When it became clear that an Islamist party would win, the army staged a coup to prevent the election being concluded. This resulted in 11 years of civil war. Is it ever permissible to remove a democratic party from power by undemocratic means?

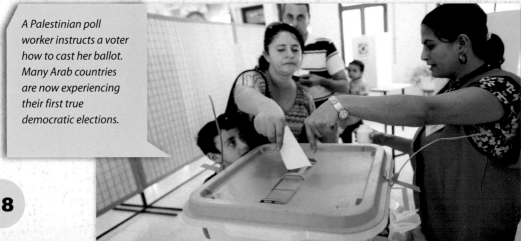

A Palestinian poll worker instructs a voter how to cast her ballot. Many Arab countries are now experiencing their first true democratic elections.

Even though his party was democratically elected, many people were unhappy with Mohammed Morsi's Muslim Brotherhood. After more protests, such as this one, the party was removed from power by the army.

'We don't want the Ikhwan [Muslim Brotherhood], and we don't want the old regime. We want a democratic state.'

Egyptian novelist Alaa al-Aswany, *The Guardian*, 2013.

DEBATE

Was Egypt's 'Second Revolution' good for democracy?

YES

President Mohammed Morsi had already reserved too many powers for himself. The Islamist constitution he was proposing was divisive. The Egyptian army has promised new elections.

NO

It was a really a military coup. Democrats should use elections rather than force to get rid of a party they do not like. The coup will discourage Islamists from engaging with democracy in the future.

FAITH AND THE STATE

The first protestors of the Arab Spring were united in calling for economic and political change. However, events in Tunisia and Egypt opened up political fault lines, which led to unrest. Should the new states be based on religious or secular principles?

'I don't support the separation of religion and politics. If you apply Shari'a in the correct way, you gain prosperity and democracy...'

Egyptian Rasha Gamal, Aljazeera's news website, 2013.

THE ISLAMIC CONTEXT

Some Muslims belong to strict sects, such as the Salafi movement, which reject the secular state. They call for full implementation of the Islamic moral and legal code known as Shari'a. While many aspects of Shari'a are compatible with a democratic state, others impact on human rights (see pages 42–43) or advocate harsh forms of punishment such as lashing or stoning, which are unacceptable in a liberal democracy. Some Western writers claim that Islam is incompatible with democracy. They talk of a 'clash of civilisations' when they compare Islamic and Western values.

Separating faith and state

Secularists are people who believe that the state should be kept separate from matters of personal faith. These people may themselves be religious or they may be atheists (non-believers). Some of them see secularism as a good thing in itself, others see it just as a practical measure to avoid religious conflict within a nation.

Democratic Islam

In reality, many different views and practices exist within Islam. Most followers of Islam regard the democratic process as legitimate, and they point out similarities with Islamic traditions, such as the key principle known as *Shura*, or consultation. Most Muslims follow their faith within pluralist systems of government.

Although the Islamists of the Arab Spring are often regarded with great suspicion by secularists, in the end both sides will have to agree ways to live with each other.

Muslim women in the Pakistani state of Peshawar demonstrate their solidarity with the Muslim Brotherhood government in Egypt, carrying banners that proclaim their support.

LIBYA, 2011-2014

In February 2011, the arrest of human rights campaigner Fathi Terbil brought protestors onto Benghazi's streets. Such events were normal during Muammar Gaddafi's rule, but these were not normal times – the Arab Spring was already under way.

The North African State of Libya's population stood at approximately 6.2 million people in 2014.

LIBYA

NEWS FLASH

Name: State of Libya
Area: 1,759,540 km²
Capital: Tripoli
Ethnic groups: Libyan (Arab and Berber descent) 97%, others 3%
Languages Arabic, Berber languages, Italian, English
Religions: Islam (97%), others (3%).
The back story:
• Independence from Italy granted in 1951.
• Muammar Gaddafi seized power in 1969.
• Gaddafi sponsored international terrorist attacks. The USA bombed Tripoli in 1986.

Libya at war

The Libyan protests exploded into an uprising, which Gaddafi attacked with helicopters and guns. This sparked off a civil war, which spread across Libya. In March 2011, the Security Council of the United Nations (UN) authorised a no-fly zone to protect the rebels from Gaddafi's air force. French and British aircraft of the North Atlantic Treaty Organisation (NATO) attacked Gaddafi's troops with missiles. Tripoli fell in August 2011.

The Libyan rebels consisted of civilians and army deserters who often had to use makeshift weapons and equipment in their battle against the Libyan army.

'They have no justification to put their hands on Libyan assets, other than as an act of theft and robbery.'

Muammar Gaddafi accuses the intervening NATO powers of seeking to profit from Libya's oil reserves, in an interview in 2012 with the Canadian *Globe and Mail*.

However, Gaddafi's supporters still held some cities in western Libya. That October, Gaddafi was hunted down and killed. He died a wretched death.

Ongoing troubles

The war was over but the problems kept coming. There were tensions between Libya's east and west. In September 2012, the US ambassador was killed when the consulate in Benghazi was stormed. Liberal governments elected in July and October 2012 failed to get a grip on national security, and militias still ruled many neighbourhoods. Prisoners taken in the civil war remained in jail without trial. The lack of law and order also created economic problems. Oil production was crippled by militia action and strikes. The promises of good times ahead remain unfulfilled.

A Libyan rebel shows the tunnel in the town of Sirte where Gaddafi was found and killed. Gaddafi ran into the tunnel to shelter from a NATO air strike.

RELIGIOUS OR SECULAR?

Should state and religion always be separated? Or can religion play a major role in government? This argument is often polarised, highlighting opposite extremes. In reality, the divisions between religion and state are often less clear cut.

The place of faith

The argument about secularism is often presented as a uniquely Middle Eastern problem. However, it is common to many faiths and most parts of the world. In Europe and North America, there are many different constitutional arrangements and various, often changing, public attitudes towards religion. Similarly, in the Middle East there is a huge difference between the strict enforcement of harsh religious laws in the kingdom of Saudi Arabia, for example, and democratic Turkey, where a moderate Islamist government works within a secular constitution.

Some Muslim women choose to wear a face covering, while others prefer not to. Should this just be a question of individual choice, or a matter of law?

These unveiled Tunisian women hold up their ink-stained fingers, which show that they have voted in elections in October 2011.

Religious freedoms

The debate poses many questions. Should religious people respect the faiths – or lack of faith – of others? Should atheists respect the rights of the religious? Should blasphemy be banned, or does the right to free speech override any offence caused? Should people be allowed to convert freely from one religion to another?

Should religious laws made by a majority apply to members of a religious minority?

For some people the answers to all these questions may have clear answers in holy scriptures, while for others they may be decided by ethical considerations. In any democracy, the laws that define a state must enable conflicting views to coexist peacefully.

'Muslims, Christians, Jews – we are all Tunisians.'

Secularist placard during Tunis protest in 2011.

ELECTRONIC REVOLUTION

The events of the Arab Spring were extraordinary because once they started, the tide of change seemed to become unstoppable. There was one explanation for this that struck many onlookers – the mobile phones in the hands of the protestors.

The rise of new technology

New communications were shaping the Arab Spring agenda. Media revolutions such as new printing technology or the rise of radio and television have gone hand-in-hand with political and social revolutions at other times in history, too.

Radical networks

During the Arab Spring, change came

THE E-SPRING

The first four months of 2011 saw the initial events of the Arab Spring. In that period:

- The region had 1.15 million people actively on Twitter, making 22,750,000 tweets. The most popular hashtags were 'egypt' (1.4 million mentions), 'jan25' (1.2 million), 'libya' (990,000), 'bahrain' (640,000) and 'protest' (620,000).
- The number of Facebook users doubled (or more) in all Arab countries except Libya, when compared with the same period the year before.

quickest in countries with the highest use of digital media. Why was this? Texting, blogging and social media sites can help in organising demonstrations, making it possible to assemble protestors in a flash. They can spread the word. Ordinary people, rather than journalists, can report and control the flow of news. They can photograph or film attacks and post them on social media sites such as YouTube.

Satellite vision

During the Arab Spring such video clips were then picked up by mainstream broadcasters. International broadcasters with strong regional connections, such as Aljazeera, which was founded in 1996, gave a voice to many activists. The Libyan rebels even set up their own Free Libya satellite station to counteract the state television channel.

Hosni Mubarak appears on Arab news channel Aljazeera the day before he resigned. Rolling news coverage kept track of the fast-changing events as they happened across the Arab world.

'In the Arab world this winter, social media proved that it can facilitate rebellion and even topple regimes... Can social media help to build new governments?'

Don Tapscott, *The Huffington Post*, 2011.

ACROSS BORDERS 2011-2014

The Arab Spring had a big impact on many nations, while lesser protests were also held in other countries, such as Algeria and Sudan. The protests had an influence on crises in other countries, such as Turkey, Lebanon, Iraq, Iran, Israel and Palestine.

Name: Kingdom of Morocco
Area: 446,550 km²
Languages: Arabic, Berber languages, French
Religions: Islam (99%), Christian, Jewish (1%)

Name: Sultanate of Oman
Area: 309,500 km²
Languages: Arabic, English, Baluchi, Urdu
Religions: Ibadi Islam (75%), others (Sunni and Shi'a) 25%

Name: Republic of Yemen
Area: 527,968 km²
Language: Arabic
Religions: Islam, small numbers of Christians, Jews and Hindus

Name: Kingdom of Bahrain
Area: 760 km²
Languages: Arabic, English, Farsi, Urdu **Religions:** Islam (Sunni and Shi'a) 81%, Christian 9%, others 10%

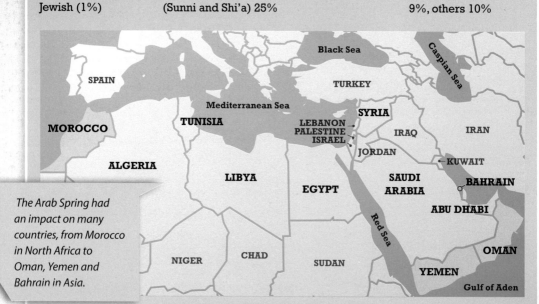

The Arab Spring had an impact on many countries, from Morocco in North Africa to Oman, Yemen and Bahrain in Asia.

Protesters in Morocco were successful in bringing about change in their government's constitution and other political reforms.

North Africa

The 20th February Youth Movement organised a series of demonstrations in Morocco in 2011. The grievances were poverty, unemployment, censorship and corruption. The king, Mohammed VI, survived by avoiding confrontation. He drew up a new constitution, made political reforms and held elections.

In neighbouring Algeria, early protests were suppressed by the police, but began to simmer again in 2013.

Around the Middle East

In 2011, crowds in Oman demanded freedom of speech, jobs and better wages and an end to corruption. They had some success: law-making powers were given to parliament, the minimum wage was raised and a job-creation scheme was promised.

In the same year, Yemen saw huge and widespread city protests, but President Ali Abdullah Saleh repeatedly twisted and turned to avoid stepping down. In June 2011, he was injured in an assassination attempt and was finally voted out in an election in February 2012.

In the small island state of Bahrain in the Persian Gulf, protests began in 2011 as calls for human rights and freedom. Another grievance was the treatment of the Shi'a Muslim majority by the Sunni Muslim government. The police response was a brutal crackdown, but protests still raged throughout 2013.

A protest march on the streets of Bahrain in 2011. The killing of unarmed protestors by security forces was to draw condemnation from around the world.

HOW IS THE INTERNET USED?

Did social media sites create these uprisings, or were they merely carriers of messages? The forces driving the Arab Spring forwards were social, economic and political, and many of the people who took part had no access to computers or phones at all.

'The Internet is becoming the town square for the global village of tomorrow.'

Bill Gates, founder of Microsoft, 1999.

Cyber-rebels

The uprisings were made much more effective by the use of new media. The media were in the hands of the younger generation. Those in power belonged to an older generation, and they failed to grasp how much the rules had changed until it was too late.

Some authoritarian countries, such as China, have tried to isolate their citizens from full access to the Internet by creating a national 'firewall'. However, the Internet generally proves harder to censor than printed media or television.

An opposition supporter holds up a laptop showing images of celebrations in Cairo's Tahrir Square, after Egypt's President Hosni Mubarak resigned.

Power games

The Internet is useful as an engine of revolution and change. However, in recent years a series of security leaks has revealed the vast scale on which national agencies are now able to intercept and monitor private media communications on mobile phones and the Internet. Does this ability to monitor communication help prevent terrorism and allow law-abiding citizens to sleep easily in their beds? Or does it allow tyrants to subdue the population? Does this massive surveillance by the state make future 'Arab Springs' less likely?

> ### '... social media will only ever be a tool of organising. The streets are the place where revolutions can create facts on the ground.'
>
> **Media commentator Sohail Dahdal, newmatilda.com, 2011.**

Protestors in Istanbul in 2013 organised demonstrations quickly using the Internet and social media outlets, such as Facebook and Twitter.

BEYOND THE MIDDLE EAST

The Arab world had been making news headlines for 100 years or more before 2011, so why was there such great interest in the events of the Arab Spring? What was so different about them?

The big players

Western Asia and North Africa had long been the focus of international rivalry. Powerful nations, such as the USA, Russia, China, France and Britain, manoeuvred to win influence, their interests centred upon the region's resources, especially the vast fields of oil and natural gas. Some of these countries have also made millions selling arms to Arab countries.

War and terrorism had left nations across the region devastated. Two troubled political arenas repeatedly threatened world peace – relations between Israel and the occupied Palestinian territories, and between Iran and the West. Neither of these problems had gone away in 2011, and there can be no lasting peace in the region until these conflicts are resolved.

A Palestinian youth waves a flag while confronting Israeli soldiers in one of the occupied Palestinian territories.

ARMS FOR THE MIDDLE EAST

Are international arms keeping the peace or encouraging conflict? According to Amnesty International, in the five years before the Arab Spring broke out, 20 nations including Italy, France, Serbia, Switzerland and South Korea sold more than US$2.4 billion worth of small arms, tear gas and armoured vehicles to Bahrain, Egypt, Libya, Syria and Yemen.

- 2010–12: The USA gave US$1.3 billion to Egypt each year to buy weapons from US companies.
- 2012: Russia announced that it would continue to sell arms to Syria despite the civil war.
- 2012: The UK sold £433 million worth of military equipment to Oman.
- 2013: A US$6.8-billion US arms deal with Saudi Arabia was announced.
- 2013: A US$4-billion US arms deal with United Arab Emirates was announced.
- 2013: The USA and UK resumed arms sales to Egypt as President Morsi was put on trial.

The popular challenge

The remarkable thing about the Arab Spring was that these uprisings threatened to undermine the whole balance of power in the region. Egypt and Saudi Arabia had always been important allies of the USA. Syria was an ally of Russia and Iran. Would the whole house of cards collapse? Would the uprisings bring war or peace? Who would it benefit?

How to respond?

The response of Western governments and media was confused. They applauded the Arab Spring, they criticised it, they supported some factions and not others, they called for democracy, they expressed concern over the rise of political Islam. Above all, they wondered if they themselves should intervene to affect the outcome.

Russian president Vladimir Putin talks to Hosni Mubarak in April 2005. The world's major powers, including Russia and the USA, have gone to great lengths to develop relationships with various Arab nations.

SYRIA, 2011-2014

Major protests began in the ancient capital of Damascus in March 2011, as well as in Aleppo and in Daraa in the south. The trigger for these was the imprisonment of some students. Within days, hundreds of thousands of people were out on the streets.

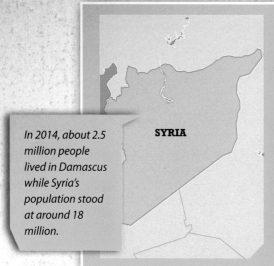

SYRIA

In 2014, about 2.5 million people lived in Damascus while Syria's population stood at around 18 million.

NEWS FLASH

Name: Syrian Arab Republic
Area: 185,180 km²
Capital: Damascus
Ethnic groups: Arabs (90%), Kurds, Armenians and others (10%)
Languages Arabic, Kurdish, Armenian, Aramaic
Religions: Islam (90%), Christian (10%)
The back story:
• The Syrian kingdom was occupied by France, which ruled until 1946.
• In 1970, Hafez al-Assad seized power.
• In 2000, his son Bashar al-Assad became president.

The long nightmare

To counter the protests, the government began a brutal crackdown. President Assad launched devastating attacks on his own cities with tanks and aircraft. Many soldiers left to join the uprising, forming a Free Syrian Army. Ceasefire bids brokered by the Arab League and the United Nations both failed. The rebels formed a Syrian National Council, but there was a growing number of small militias who had their own agenda. Both sides committed atrocities. Many foreign Islamist fighters came to join the rebels,

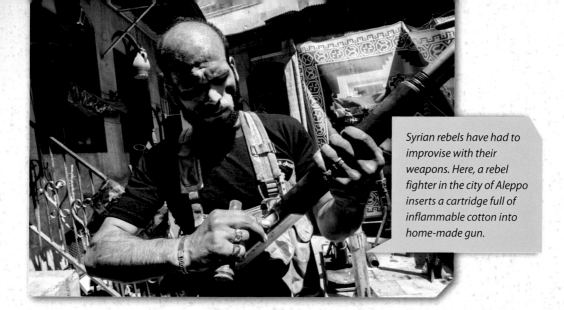

Syrian rebels have had to improvise with their weapons. Here, a rebel fighter in the city of Aleppo inserts a cartridge full of inflammable cotton into home-made gun.

who were armed by Qatar and Saudi Arabia. The Syrian government was supported by Iran and Russia.

The chemical crisis

By April 2014, over 150,000 people had died and 6.5 million had lost their homes. More than two million had fled the country. Chemical attacks took place. Some blamed the rebels, but most held the government forces responsible. One such attack in 2013 killed hundreds of civilians, including many children. Western intervention was imminent and a plan to disarm the Syrian government of all chemical weapons and

facilities was proposed by Russia. The plan went ahead. Although the immediate crisis was over, for Syrians the war continued.

Even though millions of Syrian people have already fled the country, millions more still carry out their lives amid the rubble.

'People burning in front of you. People dying. People running. But where will they run to? They're not safe anywhere. This is the fate of the Syrian people.'

Headmaster of a school hit by an incendiary bomb, Aleppo, BBC News, 2013.

SHOULD OTHER COUNTRIES ACT?

Democracy and stability are the declared aims of the European Union's foreign policy. But do Western countries' calls for democracy in the Middle East sound hollow given their history of intervention in the region?

Hypocrisy – or the real world?

Over the years, the USA and its allies have propped up dictators in many parts of the Middle East. In 1953, Britain and the USA staged a coup in Iran to overthrow a democratically elected prime minister, Mohammad Mossadegh, because he had tried to take Iran's oil fields out of foreign ownership. This act would have a lasting effect on Iranian politics.

Are these double standards that undermine the case for democracy? Or are they part of a wider move to bring peace and stability to a region, so that democracy may eventually flourish? Is there always a gap between a nation's ideals and the political wheeling and dealing it has to carry out in the real world?

DEBATE

Can democracy be imposed on another nation by force?

YES

Nations have a duty to ensure that other peoples can live free of tyranny. Human rights know no borders.

NO

By definition, democracy cannot be a 'top-down' system. It can succeed only if it comes from the people in the street.

Standing alone

A policy of not intervening in the affairs of other countries is called isolationism. In some situations it may be defensible, but in others less so. Was it moral behaviour for nations to stand by in World War II when Jews were being killed by the Nazis?

Getting involved

In the 2000s, the USA and its allies intervened in Afghanistan and Iraq. Their actions were defended because they aimed to overthrow regimes that were abusing human rights. Critics were suspicious: was it more about oil or power? In the end, both wars were seen by many as costly failures. This made some Western politicians reluctant to intervene in the civil wars during the Arab Spring.

When it comes to military intervention, should diplomacy always come first? Does intervention make a bad situation worse?

'... we have to stand with those who are working every day to strengthen democratic institutions, defend universal rights, and drive inclusive economic growth.'

US Secretary of State Hillary Clinton, 2011.

Protestors outside the White House appeal for action against Syria after the use of chemical weapons against the Syrian people.

YELAN ROHAK YA HAFEZ
MULE

COPING WITH CRISIS

What can be done by the wider world to make dictators answer for their actions, to resolve conflicts such as civil war, to encourage diplomacy or to promote human rights? A framework of international law controls the relations between states.

International safeguards

The legitimacy of any international intervention in the affairs of a nation has to be agreed by the United Nations (UN). Founded in 1945, today the UN has 193 full member states, which together form a General Assembly. Key decisions are discussed by a Security Council, whose permanent members represent the world's most powerful countries. Each member has the right to veto (reject) a proposal and this often results in stalemate and inaction. Disagreement within the Security Council held up

UN soldiers in their blue caps stand at the demilitarised zone between Syria and Israeli-occupied territory.

SYRIAN REFUGEES

The UNHCR is also known as the UN Refugee Agency. It works alongside many other UN and independent agencies to care for those escaping from the civil war in Syria.
- Lebanon has 992,000 refugees
- Jordan has 589,000 refugees
- Turkey has 668,000 refugees.

Other refugees are in Egypt, Iraq, North Africa and Europe. The UN predicts that by the end of 2014, more than half of Syria's population of 22.5 million will have fled abroad or lost their homes.

military intervention in Syria, to the anger and frustration of many. However, delay may also provide a check against over-hasty action by member states. Opponents of the Syrian proposal, who included humanitarian organisations such as the International Committee of the Red Cross, believed it would have made a terrible situation even worse.

The big picture

UN agencies deal with a wide range of the concerns and issues raised by the Arab Spring, from economic development to human rights and the care of refugees.

Multinational and regional organisations, such as the Arab League or the African Union, may also take part in diplomacy or conflict resolution. The International Criminal Court (ICC), which is based in the Netherlands, is independent of the UN and aims to bring to justice those accused of war crimes and other crimes against humanity.

Working internationally is extremely difficult and the options of all these organisations are limited and sometimes ineffective. However, without them, there would be little hope for those rising up against injustice.

'Some 9.3 million people in Syria – or about 40 per cent of the population – now need outside assistance.'

Valerie Amos, UN humanitarian chief, BBC online.

SAUDI ARABIA, 2011-2014

Saudi Arabia is the Arab heartland, its rock containing massive reserves of oil. The nation also contains spiritual riches in the form of Mecca, the birthplace of Muhammad and the most holy city of Islam, which is visited each year by millions of pilgrims. Saudi Arabia is a very conservative and traditional country.

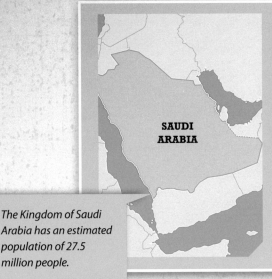

SAUDI ARABIA

NEWS FLASH

Name: Kingdom of Saudi Arabia
Area: 2,149,690 km²
Capital: Riyadh
Ethnic groups: Arabs (90%), Afro-Asian (10%)
Languages: Arabic
Religions: Islam (Sunni 90%, Shi'a 10%)
The back story:
• Regions united to form the Kingdom of Saudi Arabia in 1932.
• Oil was discovered in 1938.
• In 2005, Abdullah bin Abdul-Aziz became king. Saudi Arabia is an ally of the West, but there are concerns about Saudi terrorists.

The Kingdom of Saudi Arabia has an estimated population of 27.5 million people.

Challenging the system

When protests broke out in Saudi Arabia in 2011, they were met with arrests and shootings. The causes of the unrest were many. Corruption was widespread. While the top families were fabulously wealthy, many ordinary people were poor, and unemployment was high. Political prisoners were locked away without trial. Women were denied equal rights with men, and were even forbidden to drive cars. Women began a Facebook campaign called *Baladi*, demanding the vote. In 2011, one woman was sentenced to ten lashes,

A woman drives through Saudi Arabia's capital city of Riyadh, in defiance of the law forbidding women to drive.

having been found guilty of driving a car. Fortunately, King Abdullah overturned the sentence.

Small steps to reform

King Abdullah maintained strict opposition to the Arab Spring protests, sending troops to Bahrain to help suppress the unrest there. However, he did give in to some of the demands at home. He increased the spending on welfare. He at last gave women the vote in city elections and in February 2013, 30 women were, for the first time, appointed to the Shura, the chief consultative council. Despite intimidation, arrest and the threats of harsh punishment, the brave protestors have not given up.

With the dramatic events unfolding in Syria and Egypt, it is easy to forget that the Arab Spring has set in motion many small but significant changes, even in conservative kingdoms such as Morocco and Saudi Arabia.

Under King Abdullah, Saudi Arabia funded rebels fighting against President Assad in Syria, and gave money to the opposition to President Morsi in Egypt in 2013.

ARE RIGHTS IMPORTANT?

There is a common factor in all the issues raised by the uprisings in the Middle East. It is the question of human rights. These are the basic requirements of equality and justice that everyone on the planet needs in order to lead a happy and healthy life.

DEBATE Should all human beings have the same human rights?

YES
Human rights are universal. They apply to all people in the world equally, regardless of their cultural or religious background.

NO
Human rights are not absolute values. Their definition may vary according to the religious and cultural traditions of one's society.

Declaring your rights

Many nations have their own bill of constitutional rights and there is a European Convention of Human Rights drafted by the Council of Europe in 1950. The UN adopted a Universal Declaration of Human Rights (UDHR) in 1948. In its present form this declaration addresses many of the concerns of the Arab Spring, such as equality, liberty, security, wrongful arrest and detention, a fair legal process, freedom of thought and expression, religious freedom and the right to work for a fair wage and to education.

The UN has offices around the world, such as this one in Geneva.

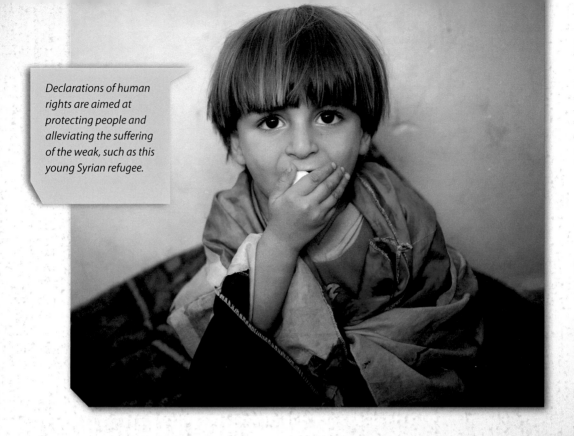

Declarations of human rights are aimed at protecting people and alleviating the suffering of the weak, such as this young Syrian refugee.

Some people criticise the UDHR, saying that it is based too heavily on Western tradition and does not allow for cultural or religious variance. In 1990, the 57 member states of the Organisation of Islamic Cooperation (OIC) drew up an alternative document, the Cairo Declaration of Human Rights in Islam (CDHRI). Based on Shari'a, it shares some common ground with the UDHR and also supports many of the aims and claims of the Arab Spring. However, it is based on a single religion and it differs from the UDHR on basic issues, such as religious freedom and equality, freedom of expression, the rights of women and the nature of punishment. These are the same issues that have often caused division between secularists and Islamists. The Cairo Declaration has been strongly criticised by the International Commission of Jurists.

'It turns out, in fact, the toppling of a dictator may have been the easy part. The difficult part is replacing that repressive regime with a rights-respecting democracy.'

Kenneth Roth, Human Rights Watch, 2013.

ON TO THE FUTURE

In 2011, young protestors in Cairo's Tahrir Square felt hopeful. They were changing the world. Today, the strife in Libya and Egypt has made many people despair of the Arab Spring. The conditions in Syria are shocking the world. Was it all in vain?

Shifting sands

The Arab Spring did upset the big power alliances across the region, and the Middle East is entering a period of change.

Many people are still living in countries torn apart by conflict or are having to cope with years of violent strife.

In 2013, it seemed that relations between Iran and the USA might be improving. However, political change is rarely delivered quickly and neatly, especially if those in revolt want all sorts of different things. Disappointments and setbacks are inevitable and violence is all too likely.

Lessons to be learned

The failures of the Arab Spring have become all too obvious since 2013. Has an 'Arab Winter' now set in for years to come? Not necessarily. Rulers who do not focus on the needs of ordinary people may now think twice about the fate that awaits them. The foundations of the Middle East have been shaken by a tremor. Many more may follow.

After the initial wave of euphoria following the Arab Spring, many countries are now facing up to the hard work necessary to bring about change.

'It is the first time we have been so united since the revolution. It is like another revolution.'

Asma Habaib, a bank worker in central Tunis, celebrates the new democratic Tunisian constitution of 2014.

GLOSSARY

Arab Spring

A term used by the media to describe the series of protests and uprisings that began in Tunisia in 2010. These protests and uprisings soon spread across many countries in North Africa and the Middle East.

atheist

Someone who does not believe in a God or gods.

blasphemy

An insult or a lack of reverence or respect towards someone's religion.

ceasefire

A break in a period of fighting. It is also called a truce.

censor

An official who blocks or alters forms of communication or media on the grounds of politics, morality, religious teaching or other concerns, such as national security.

civil war

A war fought between various factions within the same country.

constitution

The principles and legal framework on which a state or an entire nation is established and governed.

coup

Short for *coup d'état*, it is any sudden and decisive political action, especially the seizure of governing power by non-democratic means.

democracy

Rule by the people, normally through a government of representatives who have been elected by the population.

dictatorship

Oppressive, undemocratic rule by a single person, military leader or party.

ethical

Something that is based upon moral principles.

firewall

In computing, any system that vets, controls or prevents the free flow of network traffic.

freedom of speech

The right to communicate opinions and ideas easily and freely, without the threat of censorship.

human rights

Provisions or principles which aim to ensure that all humans have equal access to justice, freedom and other essential requirements.

intercept

To break into communications in order to read or listen to the message.

Islamist

A term (rejected by some Muslims) to describe the belief that Islam should determine politics as well as one's personal and social life.

isolationism

A national policy of not being drawn into any international involvement or intervention in a situation.

militia

A fighting force that is made up of a collection of citizen volunteers or non-professional soldiers.

minimum wage

The lowest wage or fee which can be paid to a group of workers by agreement or by law.

monarchy

Rule by a king or queen.

NATO

Short for North Atlantic Treaty Organisation. A military alliance dating back to 1949, which currently has 28 member states, located across North America and Europe.

no-fly zone

An area where a nation or a group of nations is prevented from deploying their aircraft during a war or military stand-off.

pilgrim

Someone who undertakes a journey for religious reasons, often to a shrine or a holy place.

pluralist

Made up of several political parties or faiths, rather than a single one.

Salafism

A movement within Sunni Islam that aims to follow the principles and practices of the earliest Muslims.

secular

Referring to matters which are non-religious.

secularist

Someone who wishes to keep matters of state or education free from religious influence.

Shari'a

The framework of principles and laws within Islam. It is interpreted in many different ways, and some aspects may conflict with secular legal systems.

Shi'a

One of the main religious groupings within Islam, in which religious leaders called imams interpret the teachings of Muhammad.

Sunni

The largest grouping within the Islamic world, in which the Ummah or wider Islamic community plays an important part.

INDEX

BEHIND THE NEWS

978-0-7502-8252-9

978-0-7502-8255-0

978-0-7502-8254-3

978-0-7502-8256-7

978-0-7502-8253-6

978-0-7502-8257-4

WAYLAND